I0517936

Other books by Serge Gavronsky
published by Dos Madres Press

Once Written-liber scretarium (2020)
A Season for Myself (2023)

For the full Dos Madres Press catalog:
www.dosmadres.com

MIND WORDS

SERGE GAVRONSKY

DOS MADRES

2024

DOS MADRES PRESS INC.

P.O. Box 294, Loveland, Ohio 45140
www.dosmadres.com   editor@dosmadres.com

Dos Madres is dedicated to the belief that the small press is essential to the vitality of contemporary literature as a carrier of the new voice, as well as the older, sometimes forgotten voices of the past. And in an ever more virtual world, to the creation of fine books pleasing to the eye and hand.

Dos Madres is named in honor of Vera Murphy and Libbie Hughes, the "Dos Madres" whose contributions have made this press possible.

Dos Madres Press, Inc. is an Ohio Not For Profit Corporation and a 501 (c) (3) qualified public charity. Contributions are tax deductible.

Executive Editor: Robert J. Murphy

Illustration & Book Design: Elizabeth H. Murphy
www.illusionstudios.net

Typeset in Adobe Garamond Pro & Beloved Sans
ISBN 978-1-962847-09-4
Library of Congress Control Number: 2024937907

First Edition

Copyright 2024 Serge Gavronsky
All rights reserved. No part of this book may be reproduced or transmitted in any form or by any means graphic, electronic or mechanical, including photo-copying, recording, taping or by any information storage or retrieval system, without the permission in writing from the publisher.
Published by Dos Madres Press, Inc.

With many thanks to

Michael Golston
&
James Sherry

INTRODUCTION

In a remarkable series of nine books published over the past fifteen years —*ANDORTHE* (Talisman House, 2007; reissued with artwork by Constance Lane by Chax Press, 2022); *Silence of Memory* (Spuyten Duyvil, 2014); *Truth Truth Truth* (Spuyten Duyvil, 2016); *Murderous Fantasies* (Spuyten Duyvil, 2017); *What's the Title? TITLE* (Chax Press, 2018); *Once Written* (Dos Madres, 2020); *Words in Memory* (Spuyten Duyvil, 2022); *A Season for Myself* (Dos Madres, 2023); and now *Mind Words*—Serge Gavronsky sets out to revise and reimagine a number of literary genres—the novel, memoir, autobiography, detective fiction, the hospital narrative, the long poem, the short monologic lyric—while in the process inventing several altogether new genres, modes, and hybrids: the "poemnovel," "an infiltration of words," "poems within a poem," a "book of secrets," "words in memory," "mind words." Employing a potent arsenal of Imagist, Objectivist, and Surrealist techniques sieved through stiff shots of Continental philosophy, Gavronsky effects what might be the most serious and sustained overhaul of the possibilities of literary production since the *Révolution Surréaliste* of the 1920's. Gavronsky honed his writing over a lifetime of translating and decades of scholarship and teaching in the French Department at Barnard College. His texts crackle with references to and quotations from people like Daniel Defoe, Wallace Stevens, Ezra Pound, Herta Müller, Baudelaire, Gertrude Stein, Thoreau, Robert Antelme, Geoffrey Hartman—these are taken from just the first five pages of *What's the Title? TITLE*—all the way to heavy theory hitters like Freud, Lacan, Wittgenstein, Sade,

Heidegger, Roland Barthes; you name it—while still managing to be uproariously funny, streetwise, and very, very heavy, if not downright dark. Anti-semitism and the Holocaust are never long out of view in his works, and several key scenes from his early life—when he was eight years old Gavronsky's family fled Nazi-occupied Europe— circulate through the texts: he writes of seeing sandbags in the Luxembourg Gardens; hearing air raid sirens while his father tells him to shelter under a table; boarding a ship for the New World and entering New York harbor; his mother refusing to live in the Bronx, preferring Manhattan: these scenes recur again and again. *What's the Title? TITLE* opens with a scene of Parisian Jewish children being herded aboard an ominous train bound for the East, their parents weeping and waving goodbye, while the French conductor checks his German-made watch and frets about the time. Arriving at their destination, "The kids are pushed off the train./In a stern,/Nazi voice,/ A guard says:/'To the / Barber!'" In a parenthetical, Gavronsky notes "(In 1941, 11,400 kids were deported, killed"). At times his poems read like dirges for the Holocaust's victims, as "We dance with ghosts/We don't know" ("The Scream," in *A Season for Myself*). But this is only one thread in a tough, dense literary fabric that is alternately somber, comical, irreverent, quirky, quixotic, earnest, and schticky, all of it mobilized by a relentless parataxis operating at a breakneck pace. The writing is difficult to describe, since it can accommodate nearly anything and in nearly any order. Much of it is set in New York City, and most of that in Manhattan, which, like Joyce's Dublin or Dickens' London, becomes the backdrop or inscape for all manner of untoward observation and desperate adventure: one could no doubt reconstruct the

City, or some Situationist collage of it, from the immense sprawl of Gavronsky's books. *ANDORTHE,* written through Louis Zukofsky's *"A"*—also a poem centered in NYC, and the entirety of which Gavronsky co-translated into French—is formally modeled on LZ's epic: figuratively speaking, it is already a poem within a poem. In its fourteen sections, Gavronsky braids short Objectivist lines into long left-justified columns, occasionally, like Zukofsky, interrupting these with letters (of recommendation, no less!) or other blocks of prose and then with "poems within the poem": short verses, the lines of which are numbered and occasionally end rhyme-schemed (ABABB, etc.), although they never rhyme! The single words "And," "Or," and "The" are periodically floated to the center of the page, where they serve to anchor and punctuate the reading. Two Interludes and an Intermission spin the text into a kind of twisting passion play of styles, quick takes, asides, and ad hoc perspectives. What happens next, however, could not be more different. Over the course of four long "poemnovels," Gavronsky constructs a series of rambling madcap epics, replete with characters straight out of a Max Beckman triptych—strangled torturers, Teutons setting out in longboats, drummers drowning out the sound of screams—organized into haphazard settings, obscure plots, and violent noir fantasies as rich and strange as anything in Dashiell Hammett or Vladimir Sorokin. The first of these, *Silence of Memory,* kicks off with the provocative question "Is this a novel?" printed in bold oversize font and positing the issue of genre that fulminates at the heart of Gavronsky's praxis. Written through Agatha Christie's *Murder On the Orient Express,* the poem…? novel…? features Christie on a book-length train ride that is interrupted by a terrorist attack, a massacre of the female passengers, and the murder of the conductor by a bevy of eight ballerinas, who cut his body in half and then "Gulped down large plastic bottles of Diet Coke." After a series of narrative detours, the last word is given to Agatha herself as she is being interrogated by a mysterious Colonel; asked to identify herself, she answers, "here's the beginning of my novel and its precipitous/ conclusion. I Smelled Bushels of Blood splattering on the table." *Silence of Memory* thus ends with the beginning (and the conclusion!) of a mystery novel, and the whole thing sputters to a close with "a memory barrier" as the omniscient narrator finds that he can no longer form a coherent memory and the prose shatters down the page in a free verse frame-breaking collapse. The three books that follow are similarly constructed: Gavronsky builds his poemnovels out of disjunctive lineated periodic dialogic sentences double-spaced down the page in loose narratives comprised of differing measures of poetry and prose that are frequently interrupted by cryptic quotations from other authors. Digression and non-sequitur are the order of the day. Catherine Silver classifies the second in the series, *Truth Truth Truth*, as an "existential memoir": formally, it is the least visually "poetic" of the books, at least in terms of its generally regular prose layout; in an "infiltration of words," its tangled, noirish plots follow characters in Berlin, Paris, and New York City. The first two sections play in degraded whorehouses and verge on a kind of snarky pornography: they read as if Georg Grosz had elected to write short stories. The third is a pastiche of memories of living in NYC punctuated with recollections of episodes from the Holocaust, the Korean War, and academic life on the Upper West Side. This volume is followed by *Murderous Fantasies*, an erotic detective story set once again mostly in Manhattan, and finally by *What's the Title? TITLE*, which, given the density of its quoted materials and the tautologically interrogative title of its recursively tautological *TITLE*, is the most scholastic and metadiscursive of Gavronsky's four books: this in spite of the fact that it ends with the gnomic couplet, "No Metalanguage./No Intertextualities." To read Gavronsky's four poemnovels in sequence is to enter a fractured, surreal world of pain, hate, anguish, and sexual and political violence, but hey, they were written during the years of the Trump presidency, when such miserable chaos was daily fare for the U.S. and indeed the world. In many ways, they most resemble Sorokin's horrific and grotesque allegories of life in Putin's Russia, hell-bent on reviving all of the terrors of WWII. Gavronsky's forays into genre-bending fiction/memoir are nothing if not prescient. But again, his restless imagination takes a turn: two of Gavronsky's next three books completely eschew the poemnovel profile and pitch brilliantly into monologic lyric. He calls *Once Written* his "Liber Scretarium," and it is indeed a Book of Secrets: eleven sections of brief, gnomic, staccato poems, wry and tightly wound, and again haunted by loss, torn memories, and war. The sheer power of the writing in this volume and in *A Season For Myself* is palpable, grounded in language stripped to the bone and under immense pressure: Pound's "*Dichtung equals condensare*" projected into an Imagist Inferno. *Season* is a prolonged ghost dance, a *Danse Macabre* of glimpses of Hell, which, as Adorno reminds us, forever wanders through mankind. These two books are downright harrowing; they are among the most devastating testimonies we have of the complex acrobatics of the traumatized mind in its ever-ongoing struggle of remembering, forgetting, and remembering yet again what it cannot seem to be able to forget: "To say they were exterminated//More has to be said,/Out loud for you to hear/Screams out there//We remember/Sitting in the light/Of memories//Darkened/When ships enter the harbor." The long middle section of *A Season for Myself*, "There Are Countless Thoughts," plays in a NYC hospital (a "Mount Sinai of the mind"), and the entirety of Gavronsky's 2022 book, *Words In Memory*, is also set in a hospital ward. Both of these works are obsessively concerned with memory, with what the helpless invalid can and cannot—or, involuntarily, does and does not— remember, caught in a tangled world of x-ray machines, needles, cold metal tables, greasy shower curtains, and doctors and nurses poking, probing, and piercing his altogether vulnerable body. Inevitably, images of Nazi torture and persecution pop up, as the hospital becomes an allegorical Theater of Memory, ghosts and names appearing unannounced from the wings and then flitting offstage, only to reappear in some dream-altered form: after all, as we've been told, every time we remember a memory, we revise it. If we can't even trust our own memories, what or who can we trust? Certainly not the Doctor or the French train conductor or the Nazi barber or the collaborationist police or any other authority figure, German, French, American, or whatever. In a passage from *Silence of Memory* that reads like an echo of another poem concerned with death and remembering, "East Coker," where "The whole earth is our hospital/ Endowed by the ruined millionaire," Gavronsky lays out the conundrum: "Say, why not consider memory a deceptive consolation, a self-imposed deception//An artful turn, a so-called void to reign over a void/undisputed?

Then an invention of a past failed, or a double/spaced fiction?//Would that satisfy an otherwise/hollowness?" The uncanny effect of this writing is that every time Gavronsky recounts—or better, re-recounts —a memory, *we remember it*: oh, there's the scene of the sirens or there's his mother refusing to live in the Bronx or there's Gulden's mustard again. In effect, the reader becomes an accomplice to Gavronsky's remembering; we also cannot forget the screams of the victims. The *TITLE* after all is not Words *of* Memory, but Words *in* Memory: what are the ongoing relations between words and memory in the immediacy of the acts of writing and reading? This is the central issue of the present volume, *Mind Words*, which is different yet again in form and shape from the writing that precedes it, but is wound even tighter to the bone and focused more narrowly on the raw nerve exposed by the earlier texts. "Mind words" are exactly what this long poem is comprised of: words sheerly *of mind*, pure imageless intellection spiraling in an intense interrogation of what it is to remember, altogether. After a few pages of the obligatory air raid sirens, hiding under the table, docking in Manhattan, etc., the writing recounts no memories whatsoever: instead, it describes in excruciating detail the immediate act of the mind as it thinks through the mechanics of memory in an ongoing account of remembering as it occurs, framed by a simultaneous interrogation of its happenstance, of what happens to it as it appears or is constructed and how that coincides with and inflects the act of writing as it goes on. And then how does *dream* operate in concert with all of this? What does it mean to "relive" something, and how does this zombie-like living again what is dead alter and distort through the very act of that "reliving," and then once again through the recording of it all? In his phenomenological existential memoir, Gavronsky explores this vertiginous spiral of mental consideration for some one hundred and forty pages in a literary *tour de force* of concentration and attention the likes of which has never be seen, written, or read: Memory Words By themselves Glaring O where Have All of them Gone A memory Replaces Places Themselves Spelling Who then Can they Catch Language will Do it Out of space There the sublime Shows my name The last fifteen pages of *Mind Words* then abruptly break from this singular linear stalactite of linguistic flow as the text spills across and down the page into broken bits of sentences, unrelated words, names of random places, and chunks of gnomic phrases, to end in a classic Gavronsky Loony Toons flourish:

"Dats all, folks!"

Happy landing if we ever can fly up your echo

THE END

Serge Gavronsky

—Michael Golston
New Mexico, January 2024

MIND WORDS

MIND WORDS

I Heard sirens
My father said
All of us
Down to the cellar
My sister and me heard
Sirens
My father
Heard

Sirens
A stream of Sirens
Father
Said
Nazi planes over
Boulogne-sur-Mer
Hitting
A Citroen
Factory
In the cellar
My father
Taught me
And My sister
How to hide

Below   DADDY DADDY DADDY
A table   You know Russian!
My father   Why are
Says   workers singing in
Nazi planes   Russian
Then

1

The next
Day
My father went
To get us
Gas masks
Then a siren

ALL CLEAR

Upstairs
Finally
I
Heard
A Biblical line
We all
Heard it
Was it a hum?
Was it to change
The tune?
At least an
                    ALL CLEAR

My father knew
A rich man from Morocco
He loaned my
Father
Enough
Money to get us
Out of France
And to dock
In Manhattan
There

A rabbi
Met us
Said
He knew
How
GREAT
My great
Great
Grand-father

Was
He gave my mother
An address
You'll be
At
At Home
In the Bronx
My mother

                                        No

My mother said

In Manhattan
My mother said
Said good
Now
We know
Thanks
To
Grand father
Times past
I don't have to

Remember
The
Details
But
Then my sister
At age 4
My teacher
Said

All of
You duck
Under
Your truly
Under
Your desks
A shower
 I heard
Words
In sadness
Always
But I knew
My sister
She too
Under her wooden
Desk
Then
An all -clear siren
The same
Over
How many
Times another
Time

I had gotten
Used to sirens

That's all I
Remember
Except
Crawling beasts
Under the
The Kitchen
My father
Killed them
All
with some kind of
White poison
Then
Somebody told
Us
Not far
From

Fort Tryon Park
All
Memories
Pushed
Into a
Background
My mother
Got a position
At the OWI
Andre Breton
Next to mother
So many

Memories
All now
Hushed

My life
Beyond a
Hush
Good Grades
Nice ties
Always
I hated
Hot cereals
A humming

I heard
Them humming a song
Out of memory
Too far to go
Words
Follow
Words remembered
Meanings
Turn
Change sights

Words alive
Words

A crowd of
Meanings

Less a thought

Less a space
A speechless
Talk unsounded
Talk out of
Memory
No sound
Of being

Silence
Please Olga I don't want
Yo
Go
To your river
Too much
Peoples
But

I'd
Love to
Read in
Your library
Besides
Venice will
Never be
The
Same OK Olga!
I prefer
Your
Venice
Library
Escaping
Anti-semites

Now
At
Some
Hospital
I can hear
Paul
Words
On
A violin
Failed
Memories
Always fail
Trying
To get to the
Do it
Fails
Only
The eyes
Glimpsed
Memory
Become
A rainfall
Filled with
Expectations

Dream-like
Sliding in
And out
Of a meaningless
Search
Say that
Again

Words soundless
By the way
Did I ever
Tell you
I
Borrowed some
Of your shelves

No   words
Here
Jumbled silence

Words
For a time of Being
Say nothing
Only the unheard
Bride of
Time
An absence
Heard an
Absence
Always
A
Repetition

To become
A silence
Remembered

Far
From itself

Outside
Unbridled
Caught a smile
Thoughtless

A banner
A hymn

A factory
Out loud
Seeking
A
Sea king
Words
Self
Couched
Near
A bundled mind
Sirens
Unspeakable
Words
Hiding
A mind at
Rest
Emotions without
Truth

Become
Invisible

Rains
The mind

On a street

Meaning
less
Words
Ecstatic
Silence
Silent words
Hiding
A breath
More of
The
Same
Mirrors
Crowded with images
Voices
Slumbering words

                              Silence

Humming words
Unsigned thoughts
Maybe
All

A tremor
bleeding thoughts
Words in captivity

Become themselves
In silence
Catch the unheard
Catalogue
Now

An invention
Crowding
A couch
But words
Reject
Words
A voice
Without
Thoughts

Getting away

                                        Thoughts

Become another

Since when
Silence talks
Silence
Harboring thoughts

There's
Always a

                                        THOUGHT

Others
Conceal
Another
An unsteady
Past or was it
Always in
Motion
Arrows of meaning
Then

There's
 Always a
Mindless
Rest couching
Absence
Only hearing
A past present

Or should it
Have been a
Consequence
A shouting silence
An elsewhere
Searching for itself
A round
Or whatever is
Voiced
Veering out of
Hearing
Around here
About
Hearing
Escaping
A voice
Not hearing
Its   selves

Then
There's always
A then

A silence filled
With
Images
A silence
Unheard
Hours after
Silence
A circle
Encircles
                                    The mind
Become another
A circular sound
A wordless
Fear
Who then
Shall speak
In a mooted voice
A round

Another
Round
Hardness breathing
                                    Silence
Thinks
Speaking
Voices
Forgotten
Yet
Heard
                                    A why
Then
A total silence

Wordless
More
Words
Stilled
Breathless
Yet
Voices remain
Then
Isn't it always
A "then"
Then what's
Unheard
Unseen

A past
Never leaves
Behind

There's always
Another voice
Hiding behind
A screamed memory
Screaming
                                        Words refuse
Words
 Escape silence
The silent
Words
Inscribing
A past
All's a
Glimpse

Waiting
Always
Or
Or
Sinking into thought
Or
Was it a
Mirror thinking
Before it

Steeps in
Sight

Whatever sound

Elsewhere
A mind on a
Boat thinking
Always a
                              Then
Anchors
Darkness
Elsewhere here an
Elsewhere
Anchors
Invisibility
                    THEN

Another thought
A pre-thought for
Light striking

Darkness

A memory
owned whatever
Soaks daylight
An elsewhere
Then
Pretends
A thought
Anchored in
Black
Then
There's always
A
Then

Multiplies
 Unknown
                          Memories
Ask
Who writes a wrong?

Unexpected
Like
A
Repetition
Glorifies
Absence
Expect an absurd
Words expecting
Below
Below

A muted
Memory
Then again a
Then

Hear
Words multiply
Always the same
Clouds
Hide
A where
When words
Hope for another
Word
Harboring
A memory
clouds
Always the
Same
As a
Breath
Hides truth
Deaths, too
Cloaking
Death

                              Nowhere

Inventing
A word
A silence
Toying
The real

Thinking
A mistake
A life asleep
As though

Darkened
Breaking daylight
A sound sleeps
Dreams a night's
Darkness
A sequence beyond
Itself
You
Cannot
Dream a
Dream
A darkness
A memory
Mailed
In words
An elsewhere
A conjugation

Airless
Spells itself in
A cloud of
Darkness
A tangible dream
Becomes a light
A sequence
A depth of
Lines

Where have all of them
Gone?
As far away as
Possible
 lights fall
Into
A sequence
Breaking silence
 passing time
Reflects light
An absence
Grasping itself
Rejecting
A line

Sleeps
In the
Depth
Of thought
Figured
Thoughts
Colors
escaping
Memory
A light
Sequence
Passing by light
In quotes
A silence
Asleep
All's silence

Only silence can
Hear its   Thoughts
A quiet
sound
Away
In a sequence
Whatever dreams
Call
Dark
Light

Silence
A sea shell changes
Passes
Time
itself
Refuses time
Only
Death survives
A
Thought
Breaches
A sequence

The same
Without punctuation

A silent
Word
All by itself
Quiets itself
Beyond thought

A silence
Once again
Stipulates
Hours of a dream
A sequence
A sequence known
Only to itself
Clothed
In a dream
Meaningless
Dream
Escapes
A quiet
Declining
Dreams
Lights the shore

                                        Dark

 Meaning

A quiet
Disposes
Light

I heard
What seemed
Like thunder
When
Streets flame

 Silence
Where are you
 A cry muted by noise

When it rains
Silence reigns in
 a bath of itself
Around water
In silence
Behaves
AS IF
Silence itself
Ran away
When nothing
Becomes
An elsewhere
There
Words tangle
Themselves
In a rain of words
Fill imagination
Flowering words
Become an
Elsewhere
Into obscurity
In a flash of darkness
Breaching space
Time beyond itselves
As if speech
Stopped talking
All spaces
Shouting
Streets shouting names
Arms raised
Streets talk
Gunfire

During days

Other words
Are in an elsewhere
Crowing thoughts
Streets of
Thoughts
Where else are they
In a night of thoughts
Shaping absence
All by itself
Crowding
Standing
Calling out
Stops

Stop everything
Students yell
Bastards
You're all
Spraying gusts
Of words

In a rain of words

Police spray

Students in
Their streets
Where else
Canons
Spray words

Students kick
Away thinking
Always in
Thoughts
Streets
What would
Harm voice
Yelling when
                    Quick words

Fly in straight
Sheets
of words
Yell when
Near death
Swells
Streets
Around wooden
Bullets
 Streets swell
When screams
Refuse
Gusts of spray

Others shouting
Water yells back
A geography
Calls voices
 Police calming
Streets
Voices
When ambulances

Spray water
Words of an ambulance
Keep screeching
There's always
Here
A repetition
Crouching
Blood flowing
Flags unfurl

                              Dreams

Expel themselves
Continue
A night
Whispering
Closes

But continues
To protect
Shouts against
Police in what
Will become
A spray of hate
Words refuse
Darkened words

Now
Sing
Revolution

Songs beheaded
Free from
Police spray
Against
Words
Asleep mirror
Pools
A past series of
Words
In hollow
Gunfire
Streets bleed
Words of
Revolution
Dream spaces
Of water
Smile
Arms raised
To the end
Shouts shoot
Dreams observe
Time turning away

Victory sings
Lights
Smile in water sprays
We'll tell our sun
Light our way

We'll check them
Out of gestures

Night dashes
Species
Water talks
Gushing
Out of depth
Where speech
Becomes   Songs
Bent
 "against"
Night talking
Yells
Water sprays
Shouts
In
Sprays
"the oncoming"

Streets overflow
Muted accusations
A barricade rains
Police aware of
Who we are
Nobody screams
Nobody cries out
Nobody yells
Here a geography
Of politics
Accompany
Brutality
Ready
Windows closed

Will they pass
Shrieks
Shrieks

A printed eye
Says
But then
I've
Forgotten
The mind
Most of it
At least a mind out of itself
Without
 Narration
Blue closes upon itself
Anchored
Then
Always a
Then
A fault sidelined
Always a
Then
An unexpected
Sleep of death
Mine
Then once
Again
Before
I wake
I see
Mine
Alone flat

On the dug-up ground
Then I say
Not alone
So many others
Some poets perhaps
A circle of flowers
Or none
Anchored in
Depth
A rejected closure

Lines
Sleep
Early rise
Will I be alone
A clear white space

Thoughts
At least
Eye me
Above
Lines
Curbed
On a near mind
Typed lines
Above
Sentenced
Below
For feet
To leave
A place
A crowd of

Words
Flowers above
Absolve time
Above
A geography
Earth
Remains
Time
Where else
A gesture
Thoughts
Pass
A dream
A line
A future line
A geography
Elsewhere
A quote
Perhaps
In sleep

You
There
Quits a thought
Repeats Itself
Again and
Again

A quotation
Another
And yet
Slowness

Will do it
Enough
As night falls
Covets a thought
A life sleeps
Below places
The earth accepts
All thoughts
Memories close
Dreams
Trying
Once again
Where have I
Been
Rolling thoughts
You too?
Rolling inventions
Refusing to
Quit
Silence
Dreaming
Close to a
Dream rejected
Sleep calls out
Where
Stacked dreams

A depth
Of thought
From midnight
To light
Rejecting

Thoughts
Above
Near Closing
Standing
Others
Standing
Her
Maker in
Tears
Then
What
Dreams
May
Become
A dream
A sequence
Even
Tears
Feet shuffle
A sequence
What else
Can dreams

Navigate?
Where else

But a
Sequence
Other graves
Where
All those feet could be
Heard

In rain
Or
In sunshine

A morning
Thought
Recalls night time
A crowd of silence
Breaks
Tears in a
Kleenex
Refusing to avoid
Reality
Where else
Does a trip fail
A morning cloud
Wiping off night
Thoughts
Unhinged
Dreaming
Always
Death
Wakes me up
Time
I did not
Squander
Sleep
Morning tells
Another
Clash in
 Negation

Somewhere where
Dreams insist
Disperse sunlight
A sequence
Always in the
Mind
Others chase another
Place
Dreams
Against
Sunlight
Again
All nights
Mirror
Each other
Disfigured
Repetitions

A silence
A sequence
Turns
Around
A pillow falls
A sleep surrenders
Holds
A dream
Always in the morning
A memory
A repetition
As if a thought
Rejected
Repetition

In the meantime

Thoughts
Reread a
Moment cries
Out in the silence
Of a dream
Yet heard
Trying
In sleep
Before
The sun rises
Over again

A dream
Where have
I nurtured
My dream
Flashes of reality
Breaking silence
Where
It can wait for
Silence

A sheet
A pillow

A mood
A sideline
Choosing
Family

I've been thinking
What
Cannot avoid the sleep
Of death a sequence
A Maternal one
Where have you
Been
A
Night
Passes

Others
Sleep
Another
Sleeps

Well filled
Thoughts

    1.   Ibid
    2.   Ibid
    3.   Ibid
    4.   Ibid
    5.   Ibid
    6.   Ibid

Well,
Like dread

The silence of a false
Sleep going elsewhere

A sound of   Sleep
Lives sleep for once

Adept
A mind gone on repetition
Trying
But at this moment

Unless…
My time is not

An idea
VS itself

Adept
Always seeking an
Escape
Trying to escape
An elevator-life
Life
Or
Was it
Death or a?
Destiny
There's always that
Possible
Escape
When that intention
Is voided
In a morning wake-up
What then is

It?
Thinking another
Track
As in writing

A draft
Please
Close all
Windows

A quiet desperation
Adept for a moment
A mile
A movement
A mind
Awakens
As in a
Dream inside
A consequence

A dream wanting
To escape
In a nowhere

To go
A misleading
Eyelash
A form of
Auto-... anything you'd like
To add!
Here's
A thought

If ever you'd had
One?

A secret secret

A sequence of realities
Brought to the surface

Of a silence
Talking
Absence
Thoughts
Adept as in an
Escape
But with no apparent
Escape

In a triangled thought
A sequence
Adept as in a dream

Death brings
Me
With it
A belief
Adept at doing
What beliefs do

To pass the time of day
A thought
Still there

Breaks time
Wherever
It might
Be

A meanwhile

After a
Thought
Trying

To break
Silence
No words will
Do it
Not yet   at this
Time
A try out
Sequences
Unheard
Here
Add
A mind
Seeking itself
Asking
Itself
Who am I
To mix reality
Within reality

A night passes by
A dream

A solitary
Preoccupation
A life adopts
A mind
In sleep
Rejects a
Thought

A repetition
A breath
Stands here
An invention
Comes
A break as in a
Moment
When the body switches
Places
A sequence
(I ain't tellin You
Anything more…)
But this is a break
What the hell
Is

Time?

Always
Boring
As in all
Repetitions?

Should it be
On another
Line?
An invention
A side steps
On a light

Adept in its own
Time

A poem decides
All's well
That begins
Well…

Too easy
Say
Something
Else
Like a
Why
Why here?

Trying out
A next line
Or two
A visit from
An elsewhere
Or a somewhere
In another
Dream half-

Awakened
Is there
Always a thought
Breaking or
Simply
Being there
An invitation
To dream

Dreaming of a

Breath a
Stop
A built-in one
Another sequence
A try out

Out
A dead

Leaf
Looks the
Other
Ways
Adept
As in a
Search
For an
Elsewhere

Yet
There's always a
There
Even in a
Dream
Miscalculates
What is
A question
Becoming
A Question
How a
Dream
Becomes
Another
Reel
Play it again
Says the dreamer

Or quitting

The light
Going always
Going
As if
To go
Was an
Elsewhere
Still
Unoccupied
In an elsewhere
Where
Dreams hear

Danger

Where
Have they
All gone?

Or was it
A thought dreaming

Going
Nowhere?
There's
Isn't
Always a
THERE?

                    Is there
Always
A dream
In another
Dream?
Then
Keep the dream
Verb will do it
Mallarmc says it with
Clarity
In quotes
In my system
I walk backwards
Wipe a thought from

My mind
Rests
Mornings will kill it
Maybe
When in my eyes
Truth partially
Wakes up
A laughing truth
Forbidden
Until words disappear
In a reflection
Doubling themselves
A prelude
Could it
Have been
Half a dream
A sequence broken
 Threads of memory
Held in
Words
As in a dream
A thought cascading
The real
Out of site
In the artifice
Of a thought
A last laugh
Still
Held
Tight
Running down
An escape

Shaping
Whatever dreams
A dream consents
To an absence
Memory
A sight a sign
Words jumbled
But never out of
Thought
A silence
Yet
Words do escape
Maligned
Doubling
Meaning
As in a machine's

Harmony
An absence
Presents when
Words
Do it
Again in the violence
Of itself
Words mangle
An invisible word
Senseless
When
Absence give words
A chance
An absence
In a downpour

Of existence

 Laughter
Parodies
A presence
Without words
Filled with
Contradictions
Filed away
Talking by itself
A downpour
Words escaping
But the mind dreams

Placated
Words

Waiting for a
Meaning dispersed
In a moment's fatigue
Columns of repetitions
Talking where dreams
Once talked
A hesitation
Rivaling
Dusk
Words allow
Themselves
To breach silence
When it becomes
Memory's times
 A circle

Timed

Hearing time
A fearful
Time
Written
Now
Memorized
What is to come
A mirror talks

 Circles shape
 What's
To come
Huddled
In fear
Where sounds
Continue to write
Watching themselves
Turn into
Words
In the light
A darkened tunnel
A reflection rivals

Words
Memorize
When a gulf
Sinks
Only

Leaving a type
Of thought
At the crack of
Dawn
What then is to become
A mirror
Shreds its
Light
Outside
Words
Say
A memory stabled
In a morning light
A dim place in
A horizon
Shadowing thought
To come
An explanation
Light
Thoughts
In fear
Under the light
Circulate
A thought
Rivaling
A thought
Hides
Light
Casting
Treading space
A language
Thought

Infinite
Questions
But where's
Language
Read what is
To come in
Silence
In a whisper
Saying
Who am I
A far-sighted
Goal
Lights
Darkness
Until
Dust
Crowds
Meaning
On an abandoned
Stage
Dreams
Too close to dreaming
Caught
Drawing
Words
Dimmed
In a car's
Headlights
At dusk
Dreamed ahead
A fear
Constantly

There
At dusk
But in a flight
Dreams
Only
Shapes
Sounds
Rivaling
When it becomes
Other than
Itself
Blinded
By memory
Headlights
Celebrating
Dusk
Becoming
Its own
Circular time
Wavering
Who watches
Time reeling
Casting aside
The logic of time
Watching
As it disables
Thought in a
Dream
Trying to arise
In a new
Geography
Watching its

Truth
A geography
Without
Images
Then a bracelet
 A circular time
Blinded
By itself

You too
Whisper
Absence
On the look out
In a reflexion
Asks then
What is to come
Perhaps a circle
Widening
Suffering words
Almost choking
You
Dimmed
In a circled time
Listening
Mouthing
Words
Refusing
A passage
A harrowing time
A circle
Breaching
The impossible

Explosion of
Words
Sounded in
Silence
The silence

Of memory
Rejecting
Dreams
Lost in the mouth
Tasting
Time
Circular time
All quiet
As a dream waking up
Out of a circular
Time
A flight
Out of
Time
Rejected
In the smell of
Time
Watching
Itselves
Cornered
As
Forms of a
Dream waking
Itself
Watching
Time going

Back in time
Sounds remember
Sounds
Hear
Themselves
In fear of
Language
In a mouth
Nearly
Swallowing
The sound
A voice
Speechless
A reflexion
Of itself
A fear
A death
In the eyes
Of a mouth
Mumbling
Time as a
Sequence
Where
Then
Can I escape
What you call
The real
A desolate
Meaning
What is to
Come
Headlights

Hearing
Words
Splash
Meaning
A reflection
Yours truly
Lights
Draining
Sense
Who then
Will hide where
Your thoughts
Cast a verb
A light
In a
What is to
Come
When

Mankind escapes
Logic
Dust of words
Casting shadows
Past
A thousand
When thoughts
Are prisoners
Hiding
A constellation
Buried
In the sound
Of memories

Close
To silence as
Meaning

But a sequence
Makes it up
A reel of thoughts
Caught
For a time
Being
A flip of a
Coin
Before
A flame dies
Seduced
Wearing
A mask
Or a
Heart
Or on a sleeve
Thoughts
Once hidden
Revel in sadness
How far
Can words
Take you
Reading
A mind

A body at rest
Paroled
Thoughts it was

Nothing ever
What it seemed to be
Defaced
Denied
What seems
True as a thought
Garaged
When the sun
Rivals a thought
Declining
A thread of being
Elsewhere
When my mind disturbs
A line of words
A Mozart concerto
Seduced by
Itself
An artificial thought
Flips a coin
Wherever it
Lands

On a couch or a
Folding chair
Listening
To itself
Meanings
Untouched
Paroled in
Silence
Words
In disbelief

Listen
To a colorful
Guitar
Hiding
Thoughts
A voice
A sleepless
Voice
A fear of
Silence
Of an absent
Breath
Gone
A thought
Gone
Paroled in a
Foreign language

A cavalcade
Waking up
Thoughts
In colorless
Words
Flipping a thought
A glowing sound
Where
Have they
All
Gone

Refuses to reel in
Reality

Strings

Of thoughts
Hiding from
Themselves
As a thought
Fails
To manipulate
Thoughts
An elsewhere
Frightens
Reality
Refusing its
Reality
Paroled
Elsewhere
Stop flipping
Thoughts in
Pillows
Repeat
Stability
Where
Or
Where
Have all of
Them
Gone
Turning
A thought
An early
Morning shadow talk
Quite clear

Now
Hidden
In an artificial
Storm
Where
Words
Change
Words
Paroled
Behind
A thought

Let night dispel
A decision
A dream
Fearful
Imprisoned
A mask
A real

Facing reality
Flipping a truth
A mind reeling
A displaced thought
In anguish
Refuses
To admit
The
Inadmissible
Call it
Death
Too short

A word
Then
Let a somewhere
Decline a verb
Stilled
Not even tracks
Leave
A shadow
Playing a mind's
Guitar
A paragraphed
Thought
Gone somewhere
Far from a
Where
Where have they
All gone
Sounds in
The mind
Flipping
Thoughts
Inadmissible
As in a flip of a coin
Defaced
Now
Unknowingly
Lying to itself

Who wakes up the dead
Out of an imaginary
Sleep
Seduced by light

Uncovers
A fisherman's
Net
Dreams caught
In an ambush
A neighbor rejects
A mirror thought
Blocked by
Daylight
Or was it a
Simple
Thought
Unrolled
Like a cigarette
Close to
Death
A dream
Enough
To wake up
The sounds
Of a voice
That is
Still
Not even
A shadow
Spells reality
Without a
Mirror
Was that
A gag order
Tells my dream
A Reality
All gone

Hiding a thought
The mind's
Invention

A crossword
A game of
Thoughts
Faces up
A currency
Yet spent
Out of
A silence of
Being
One next to
Another
Shape of thoughts
Opening a door
A silent memory
Invented
A refusal
Always ahead
Of itself
A morning

Nightmare
An invention
Clutters
Words
But who holds
The secret of
A dream
Of thoughts

A jumble
An escape
A distance of
Thoughts
Invented
Anything
To
Salve one's
Life
In a moment
A thought
Dripping away
A thought passing
Beyond itself
Beyond the silence
Of memory
Dreaming words

Against the poison
Of thoughts
Gags
Itself
A refusal of
A sublime dream
Out of the kingdom
Of the real
Reeling a thought
Again
An invention
A drink
From the realm
Of truth

An invention
A
drive
Through a
Park
On a
Week-end
When reading
Mirrors
A truth
Seeking itself
Out of gag orders
A truth says
Climbs
A carousel of
Thoughts
Heard rounds
Dispelled
Crossing out
Silence
Barely heard
Then
More of a singular
Measure

Dreams invent
Themselves
Out of wordless speech
A vocal gesture
A breath
Held in the
Mouth of

Truth
Out of the silence
An imaginary
Memory
Pleats
Of reality
Sounds
Of reality
As it seems to
Be
Or an
Invention
Hampered
By memory

A dream
An elsewhere
A repetition
Confounds
Itself
Echoes itself
Themselves belonging
To an echo
A shredded
Dream
Not even
A hand
Reveals itself
Crossing
A bridge
A float of

Tears
A holiday
Children
Accompany
Parents
Smoking
Tears of long
Ago without
Memory
In a quiet part
Of memory
For time itself
An invention
A solitude
In the quiet
Of a passage
I cannot remember
The beginning of
The end
But I wait
For answers
On the watch
Seeing myself
Ordering time
Listening
Inventing
What
Seems outside
When my eyes

Close

Curtains
On
Myself
So far
A cloud
Dreams
Places

In an Elsewhere
A hidden
Memory
Dispels
A sad
Day dislodged
Like
A nightmare
Where can I be?
Probably
A multiplication
Or could it
Have been
A repetition
A distance

From what
Was
To where
It shall be
An immigrant
Face
Covers
A fear of

Death
Shuffled
In time
A place
Half darkness
Where memory
Switches
Tracks
Where did it
Go
A where
Yet to be
Captured
By thoughts in a
Dream

Better
Than
Myself
When my doubts
Curtain
Myself

Ahead of its
Time
Partially
Shrouded
Voiceless
A place inside

A whisper
Pushes away
A night
Disturbed by
Itself
Where dreams
Travel
Was that
Always
The same
Or
Another
Falls into
Language
Ahead of all
Day nightmares
Then
Calls out
Dreams
A failed
Death
A thought
Dismembered
Parts of me
Lost on a
Trip
Isn't it
Always
The same
Caught
In a net of
Thoughts

Whether
A day
Shoved aside
Saved for a
Profile
Speechless
Thought
Yet
To be a thought
Claimed
Isn't it always
A repetition
Or
Something like
Itself or should it be
Themselves as always
A within
A without
Caught in
Tears over
                              Biography
Yet
Dispelled
Beyond
Itself
Asking
Always
Asking
Where
Is my
Voice?
Lighting the way

Fearing
Light
Sliding
Away
Ask
O! where
Where
Have I gone
Passed the light
Shuffled in
Darkness
Shrubbed words
For now
Dispelled
Maybe
An elsewhere
Caught in a

Light
A place of
Darkness
Hiding beyond
A mirror
Where am I
A repetition
All that's left
Words
Thrown aside
Where
Did I

Go?
Beyond
My dreams
Runaway
Thoughts
But
I can't

Suppress
Myself
Eros
Keeps a
Syntax
Sublime
Tense verbiage
Gone away from
A prison of
Memory
Of halting thought
Even
Language

The return of
Boredom
Read says
Pascal
Hop a Hope
Sneeze hopes
In slight
Degrees of
 Gestion or

A gesture
Out of
Thoughts
Shuffled an aside
Dispelled
But
In the stillness
Of a place
Beyond words
Into
An elsewhere
Caught
In sounds
another language
Estranged
Mind closed
Windows

Still
Caught in
An always
Away from
Fragile place
Words
Cannot
Like elves
Punish
Lives
There
In the light of day
Climbing

Still far from
A sequence
Away
Hiding
Somewhere
Sounds
Where have all
 All of them
Gone into
An invention
Invented
In rivers
Of
Questions
Still here
To be
Yet
True to a truth
Questioning
An elsewhere
Under an artificial
Light
Could it have
Been
A way
underground
Thrown away
Crossed by
Water
In the fire of
Day
Registered

Born here
On 12 scales
Devoured
In a mind's pencil
A mobile face
Speech
Shuffled away
After an Unnamed
Yet
As figures of
Speech
Asleep
An always
There
Inescapably
There
Memory
Words
By themselves
In spates
Glaring
Where
O where
Have
All of them
Gone
A memory
Replaces
Places
Beyond
Themselves
Spelling

Who then
Can they
Catch
A space
Language will
Do it
Out of space
There the sublime
Shows my name
But I've
Forgotten where words
Flight of words
A round of strings
Theory and
Practices
A straight line of
Words
Pushed aside
Where have all of them
Gone
Probably
To an
Always
Into
An elsewhere
Looking
For a distance
To propel words.
Into
A where
Or an
Elsewhere

I cannot see
I cannot
Beyond
The invention of Words
Precision
How difficult
Living in words
A length of time
Waiting for the
Invention of
Time
Less time
A body's work
Inventing
A body
Seeing others
On a scale
Climbing
Out of
Sight
Eyes still staring
When cards

Flip
How sad it was
To live languages
As if a pit
Lacking breath
Cheered
An abstraction
A way
Wafted away

Hearing always
Hearing
Time's
Syntax
Women of Trachis

As far as
 6 7 8 9 10
Theatre
Pushing
The
Same thought
Images
Calling
Anger at itself

Rejecting
The invisible
All of it
Hiding
A shadow
Asking where
O
Where
Have I
Been mocking
Truth
As a mountain
Climber
Impossible
Ask Robinson
Crusoe

To climb
What he saw
Telling
Thoughts
Impossible to

Syntaxable when days
Give way when
Lights fade
Into typography
There
There are no more
Intrigues
But
What subway
Should You
Imagine
Lines of
Paragraphs
Of the same as if
A curtain had
Fallen
On myself
Speechless
Impossible sublime
Language buried
Waits
To word it
Out of
Memory
Recapitulating

What's left
The stanza on
Piano
Perfumes
Concealing
An inadmissible
Truth in
Stealing
Looking for
Wordly words
How simple
How telling
How negation
Sweeps across
Horizons of the mind
They too
Fail to
Orchestrate
Remembering
What is
Beyond
Beyond of or in
UR
Memory
Rises
A memory
Of orchestral
Unassailable

In a lapse of
Memory-time
Where

Have
I gone
To a distant land
As near as it can be
Where
Memories drown
A collection of
Dreams
Silenced stanza
Waiting for syntax
As in a broken
Speech
Of houses of
Words
Time of
Lines
Stanzas
Every language
A metaphor
An invention
Or
An invention
Ibid

Anal
Ibid
Days anguish
What's the
Time
Ibid
More ibids
Finziu,

le pere anal
Singing anal
Grounding
A hesitation
Blocking survival
In a sunset
As words
Anthropologies
Creep out of
A linear memory
As words
Deep in the darkness
Memory
Haggles over
An invention
Time
Of words

Barely audible
A price
Other words
Misspelled
As if
A sentence
Could be
Beyond itself
Sliced out
Of itself
Trying to do

The same
In semi-darkness

Breathing
A difficult breath
Draining dreams
Where
Where Can I
Be
A disabled
Question
A body no longer
Beyond
Reflection
A face
Mirrored
In the sound
Of kids playing
Letting
Words
Play

Holding a
Breath
In a moment
Disables
Time
Discovers its
Memory
Hears a
Quandary
Its going to return
From childhood
To a now
Nervous

Shadows
Of my memory
Remain
Signals of memory
Difficult
As if
A passion for
Itself
Motions
As if

Words
Could draw
Meanings
A score of
Meanings
Death itself
Cloaks
Voices
Searching
There are
So few
Words
Hear

Scorched
On a dead land
Forgotten
Words
As if
Language
Could

Wear a Mask
Disturbed
By language
Nibbling a truth

A survival
An absence
Elementary
Structure
A sleep thought
Calculates
Where
O where
Have all those
Words blame
Blame
A series of
Words
Shapeless
At least
On the piano keys
This time
Always as time
Goes by
Sailing
Out of
Mind
Words
Momentarily
Then
Flood
Faces

Words
Hiding thoughts
Unclaimed

Rejected
Exchange
Fearing
The nameless
Coupling
With words
Near a
Plunging
Breasts disturb
A thought thinking
How to reclaim
A memory's recent depth
Searching
For words to do
The same trip
Currency times
Time out or ever
But time
Remains beyond
Time
For a
Non-structural
Calculates
How far
Words in a reject
Hide
Documents

In the garbage of time
A gloating past
A place
All thoughts
A pleasure Remembered
What else
Could they
Do?
A mind
Hides
In a
Paragraph
Seeking
What follows
A guitar
A blue space
Where words
Double themselves
In an endless
Paragraph guitar
Hiding

From itself
A beyond
Always a
Beyond
A sound
Withers
A here else
 Going
Thoughts shelter
A philosophy in a

Bedroom
A surgical dream
Calculates a never
Never
Lands into
An elsewhere
 An absence
Calculates
A forever
In a
Chorus
Bypasses
Calculates
Itself
Leaving
Straying
Thoughts
Meaningless
Where have
All of them
Gone
Elsewhere
Says it again
Elsewhere
Rallying
Memories
A cigarette smokes
Dislodges
A thought
Still playing
Colored
Memories

Playing close to a
Grave
Words kept
In a lost word

Straws
Phantasms
35
36
37
38
A load
Tertiary
Where

Have they all
Gone
Forgotten in
Sleep
Penalties
Non-fiction
A sudden flight
Dreams
A DREAM
ZUKOFSKY'S
APOLLINAIRE
DREAMS
A DREAM OF
What is heard

Distances
Sequesters

Reality
Reeling
Far from
The herd
Leaves
Lurching
Thought
Cigarettes stamped
Foot on the grass
Wheeling
Thoughts
Weep
Where
O where
Is hidden a thought
A place Where

Tears spray earth
Flowers
Shatter
Their assignments
A secret passage
All of the earth
Pounded by
Fear
Crying
Spacing
Memories

Of another visual
Memory

A movie in need of
A memory passing words
Words bring up
Time
I said movies
When I was young
Close to Broadway
Afternoon darkness
Pop Corn
Maybe
A soft Drink?
Then a train of
Movie memories
Again
The Olympia
Then
Downtown
Riverside
And
The Beacon with a
Stage opening
An orchestra
On the right side
An organ

All Jews from Europe
Either dead
Or once again
Playing music
First
At the Beacon
Then

In Hollywood

Listening how
Memory works
Words

Then
Words
Disappear
A white screen
A rush
A Toilet
Rolls of paper talk
Now
An end why not
Say   ends

I hear
You
memories
Crowd words
They could have been
In Russian
In French
In English
Docking memories
In the words of another language
Still
Waiting

For words

To read horizons
Die
Nacht
Tage
Kamen und mit ihnen die entsetzlichste
                              Gewissheit
                              Meines
                              Lebens

Was ich für eine lokale Sache gehalten hatte
Sollte eine allgemeine
                              Revolution
Sein
Bay head
Point Pleasant
Belmar
Lone Branch
                              Maintenant n

Secaucus
Perth
Amboy
                              Allons enfants
                              De la patrie

Interface   Against
                        Itself Then

Gallimard
Death of
Sollers
                              Asks
                              Where is
An arc

Knows

Bodies

Here

Allons

Enfants
De la Patrie
Serious dish   75 Paris smiles
The most striking word

A reeling we will go
Horses
Eyes   Reel
Interface   Logique
Against La mort
Holy
Cross
Contre la

MORT

Poet critic bashing   Words
Wooden faces

Coast   Along
My transitory   Narration
Troubles a head
Eyes
His mouth spoke

I forget

What's up
A

Sliver off third   Base sleeping
Off Third
Avenue
Or   would
                                                    Le Voleur

      A sister
                                                Hides

Ha!
Au revoir
L'auteur est   Le Voleur

To Harry halls

Mouths
Horses gaping
A poem

On
A
Visual   POEM
Aint
Brooklyn   A
Shadow Writes
Walt   Where
Have
                                  I been

Straight a heed
                                  Raises

A cycle
Three
Wheels

                            Rent a
Corpse
Over   Brooklyn
                            Past

Or
Was it a   Prick
                            He

Motions
Drinks   Cries
Raises a Star
Past

                               Word
                               In

Anger
Name Brooklyn
Raise your

                            Elbow

Soon
I say

                            You'll

Say
Save
Brooklyn   Hits
Yours truly
Where have you   Been
Is it for   Nothing
He says
Friend cycles   in

In a Now
Moves

                            Pedals away

Was it
                              All for
Rien
                              Build a
Bridge
          Exclamation   Point

                    Keep moving
One
Dies
                              On the
                              Way

Pier there's
You
I   write
                              Zum coffee

All's
An
End
                    ON
A cycle
All
For
No

Thing harms a bike
Dies
On

Road there's a   Poem
Noises   In a mouth

                                        Chew
Then
Rest
                        Straight as a
BIKE   No name
All for   Nothing
Then   But a
Funeral song   recites a Poem
Ride a bike past
Words   Lost
In
Words   Are their
Bikes dead
On the   Road

Newark
All is quiet on   A western
A Western   Flies
Frontal fuck
On a spring
A good day
For the earth
Raises   A tear
Near saw a dead   Men scatter
Reflections
Uptown
Now   here

                    Ich
                    Hatte
                    Schon
                    Immer

                                                    101

Gewusst

Dark chocolate
Light my car's pumping words
                        Tomber
                        Boy you
Aint seen   More
Baby
Says Wittgenstein
Gotta
Swing a word
Dark chocolate
Light me a
Cigar
                        To fall
                        Ha
ving
To boast
To feed words
The same or
Others
Mean   ing
Bang bang
Haste hangings are all
Nice
To
Watch
            What's the
Time to eat
Indian words

Sans drinking Alcohol
In solitude
Feud
Freudian
To feed
Fire.
Now
Bottom writes
Zukofsky
Hoist
All is
All

                  Ok!
              Gimme a
              Break
              To pull

Whatz
De
Nightmare   Riding
Fire
Foot
              Tonto
Says where's   My buddy
Flinch
Hoist
Halls equal hall

                  The
Manchurian collection
Mama's Book of the

                Dead

Guess what's
To follow
                          A Tisket a
                          A Tasket

All is a
Transfer
                          On the skin so far
Worlds will   Do it
                              Mallarme

Dozes
Do sit down
Response says   He
Writes
Pour Stephane   Mallarme

                          Join

tdf
www.tdf .org

                          "A"
                          Vision
Of
Cody
                          So he

Never
Had an
Introduction by Allen Ginsberg
So…And

Goody   Goody

I say
Double your BRAIN

                 Quiet commutation

Shelf the
Unwanted   Elephant Boy Scouts

"A"   Section 12
 B   Baby

              Condolences
Will a will die quid pro quo
Here's a
              Circle
Entails
             12 tables

Essen
For breakfast
             945
             12 43
             Got time
In a fruit for a   Quicky

"A"
Section
                                "A"

DOO DOO

Gib me a
             Circular
Skip the ice creamy

Airy spells airy airy
Spells Egyptian
Hold on a
Book   Repeat   Book
Hear now
Hear
Again words on a
Motion
Who will   Juggle
          My
Words
Waste them when a moon
                             Blights
Fingers of the
                             Word
Draw a circle then
                             Here:
Mallarme.   Les mots
                   Anglais

To hail
To feed
To heed
To spit

To itch   To fire
                             To feed

Then…
Add news from
Home
Education
Publications

In Tetrameter

                  Write

Call Phono/graph
Then draw an

            analysis   OOOOO
Old English
Freedom to
Feed what's next:
Versification   Naval combat   HA
                        HA

Got you   Now or never
                  In this embedddded
Laryngal   Alliteration in Naked Wolf
All is a reduplication
                Close the
                Circle
Add: www. Orgasm   Great eggs for

Breakfast
Prisoner   Catch if you
              If you can catch
 Soup of the journey:
             Optimality
Och
Alliterations if you   Make it flow

Join   Full time out

An Eskimo

Speaks up!

       Against futurism or   Fiction
As in a wash stand

Kafka says: Against forgetting the twentieth Century OK?

But, there is always   The Gnostic but who Is
The son of
Super super couple in the Bathtub

Reduplicating all that follows, let's
Say:
There maybe
Cold air or
You've just
Off twenty minutes of your

LIFE

Dats all, folks!
Happy landing if we ever can fly up your echo

THE END

ABOUT THE AUTHOR

 SERGE GAVRONSKY, born in Paris, now lives in New York. He was educated at Columbia University, from where he received his PhD in European History. He subsequently held the position of Professor of French Literature and Poetics, at Barnard College, Columbia University.

He has published eleven books of poetry in French and in English, in addition to over twenty artist's books in France. In English, he published poetry, fiction and literary criticism, as well as five books of translation of contemporary French poets: POEMS AND TEXTS, THE POWER OF LANGUAGE, TOWARD A NEW POETICS, SIX CONTEMPORARY FRENCH WOMEN POETS, THE WRITING OF APPOLLINAIRE. His main focus was the poetry /poetics of Francis Ponge.

His last major publication in French, in 2020, was Louis Zukofsky's "A", co-translated with Francois Dominique.

He is presently writing a new work of poetic fiction.

His more recent publications include: SILENCE OF MEMORY, TRUTH TRUTH TRUTH, MURDEROUS FANTASIES, AND WHAT'S THE TITLE? TITLE, ONCE WRITTEN, published by Dos Madres Press, ANDORTHE, Chax Press, WORDS IN MEMORY, Spuyten Duyvil.

Author photo by Susan Kuklin

www.ingramcontent.com/pod-product-compliance
Lightning Source LLC
Chambersburg PA
CBHW021649120626
46545CB00002B/780